Libélulas

Grace Hansen

ABDO
INSECTOS
Kids

www.abdopublishing.com

Published by Abdo Kids, a division of ABDO, P.O. Box 398166, Minneapolis, Minnesota 55439.

Copyright © 2015 by Abdo Consulting Group, Inc. International copyrights reserved in all countries. No part of this book may be reproduced in any form without written permission from the publisher.

Printed in the United States of America, North Mankato, Minnesota.

072014

092014

 THIS BOOK CONTAINS RECYCLED MATERIALS

Spanish Translators: Maria Reyes-Wrede, Maria Puchol

Photo Credits: Shutterstock, Thinkstock

Production Contributors: Teddy Borth, Jennie Forsberg, Grace Hansen

Design Contributors: Candice Keimig, Laura Rask, Dorothy Toth

Library of Congress Control Number: 2014938850

Cataloging-in-Publication Data

Hansen, Grace.

[Dragonflies. Spanish]

Libélulas / Grace Hansen.

p. cm. -- (Insectos)

ISBN 978-1-62970-334-3 (lib. bdg.)

Includes bibliographical references and index.

1. Dragonflies--Juvenile literature. 2. Spanish language materials--Juvenile literature.

I. Title.

595.7--dc23

2014938850

Contenido

Libélulas

Las libélulas son insectos.

Las hormigas, las mariposas

y los escarabajos también

son insectos.

4

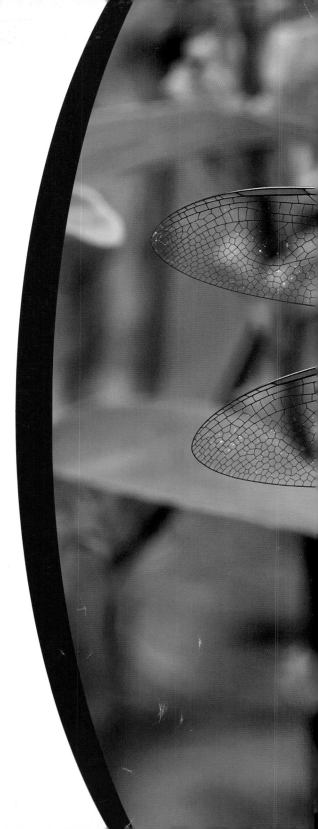

5

Hay libélulas en casi todos los lugares de la Tierra. Se las ve **frecuentemente** cerca de lagos, estanques y **arroyos**.

Las libélulas pueden ser de muchos colores. Algunas libélulas son peludas.

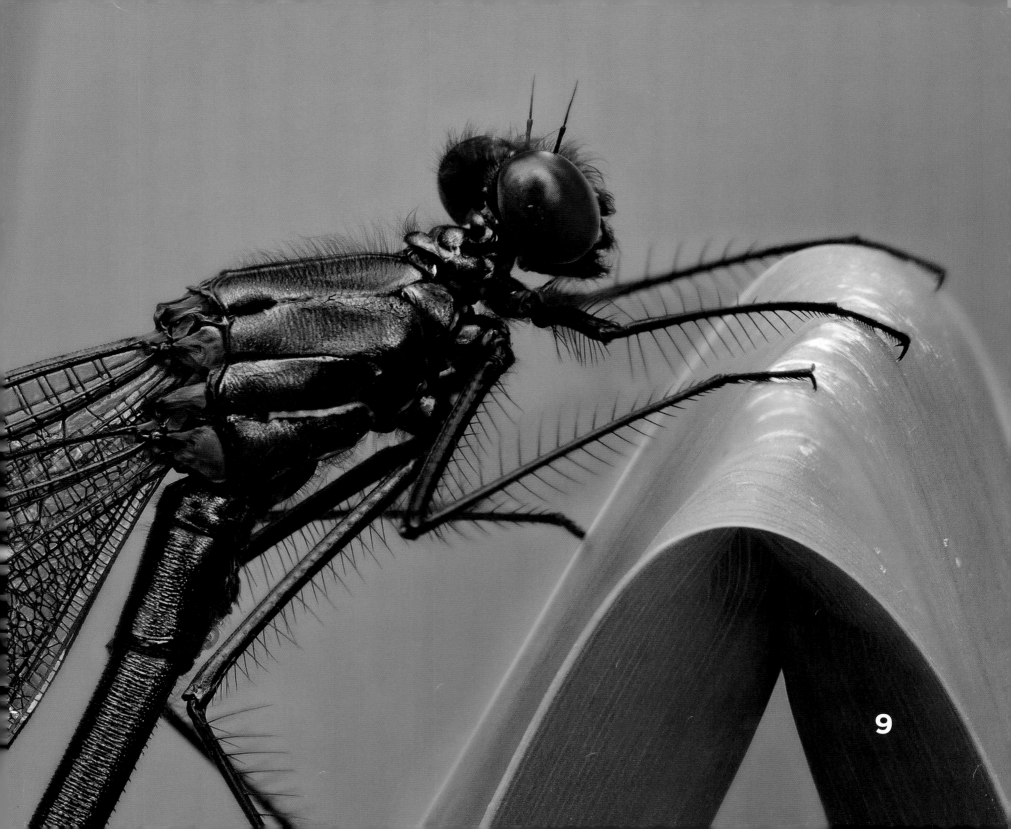

9

El cuerpo de las libélulas tiene tres partes principales. La cabeza, el **tórax** y el **abdomen**.

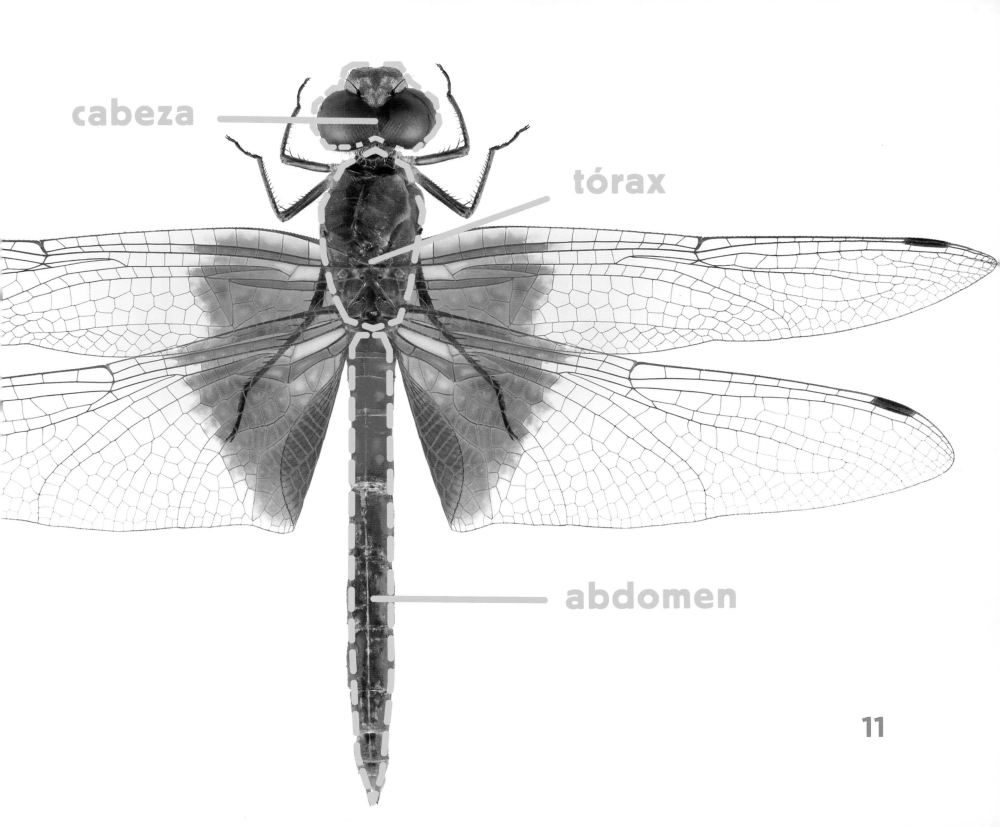

cabeza

tórax

abdomen

11

Las libélulas tienen seis

patas y cuatro alas.

Tienen dos ojos grandes.

13

¡Las libélulas pueden volar rápido! Sus alas les permiten volar en cualquier dirección.

Caza

Las libélulas son buenas
cazadoras. Les resulta fácil
atrapar a sus **presas**.

16

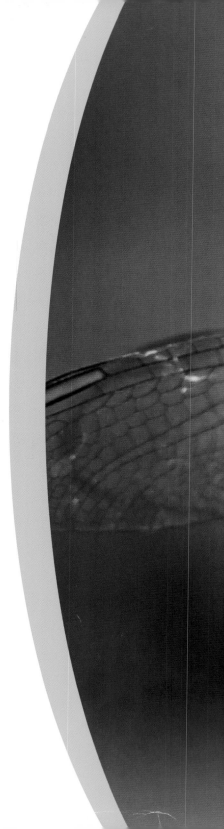

Alimentación

Las libélulas comen
pequeños insectos,
como moscas y mosquitos.

19

Las libélulas ayudan al planeta Tierra

Las libélulas son alimento para otros animales. Los pájaros, patos y peces comen libélulas.

Más datos

- Las libélulas viven desde hace millones de años, mucho antes que los dinosaurios.

- ¡Las libélulas prehistóricas podían medir hasta dos pies y medio (762 cm)!

- Las libélulas macho se pelean para defender sus casas.

Glosario

abdomen – parte trasera del cuerpo de un insecto.

arroyo – pequeña corriente de agua.

frecuentemente – muchas veces, normalmente.

presa – un animal que ha sido cazado por un depredador para comérselo.

tórax – la parte del medio del cuerpo de un insecto.

Índice

abdokids.com

¡Usa este código para entrar a abdokids.com y tener acceso a juegos, arte, videos y mucho más!

Código Abdo Kids:

IDK0403

It was a beautiful day.

For Tony, who has been Jack the Bear for many people, for many years

Artist's note:
The illustrations in this book were done on recycled paper shopping bags. I used watercolor, crayon,
and almost every ballpoint pen, marker, and pencil I could find in my desk's untidy drawers.

First published in 2009 by Simply Read Books www.simplyreadbooks.com

Text and Illustrations © 2009 Christina Leist

LIBRARY AND ARCHIVES CANADA CATALOGUING IN PUBLICATION
Leist, Christina
Jack the bear / Christina Leist, author and illustrator
ISBN 978-1894965-95-8
I. Title.
PS8623.E477J32 2008   jC813'.6   C2007-905129-4

We gratefully acknowledge for their financial support of our publishing program
the Canada Council for the Arts, the BC Arts Council, and the Government of
Canada through the Book Publishing Industry Development Program (BPIDP).

Book design by Elisa Gutiérrez

10 9 8 7 6 5 4 3 2

Printed in Singapore

Jack
the Bear

by Christina Leist

SIMPLY READ BOOKS

Nosy Fox was strolling through the forest when he spied Brainy Owl perched in a tree.

Under another
tree, a distance
away, sat a bear
that Nosy Fox had
never seen before.

"Who's that?" asked Nosy Fox.
"That's Jack the Bear," said Brainy Owl.
"Oh? And what's he doing?" Nosy Fox was,
well, nosy.
"He's making the world a better
place," replied Brainy Owl.

"Really?"

Nosy Fox smirked. "He looks like he's just sitting in the shade with a jar of honey."

"Take a closer look," said Brainy Owl. "What do you see?"

Nosy Fox looked. "He's giving Grumpy Squirrel some honey.

HOW does **that** make the world a better place?"

"I thought," said Nosy Fox, twitching his tail, "that making the world a better place was a job for kings and queens and presidents and prime ministers."

"Oh, it is,"
said Brainy Owl.
"But sometimes they
bite off **MORE**
than they can chew.
They can't do **everything**.
They need Jack's help."

Nosy Fox huffed. "What about the scientists? Don't they help the leaders by coming up with **important** ideas?"

"They do invent incredible things.

But it takes more than inventions

to make the world a better place. That's where Jack comes in."

"**Well,**
what about all the
peace prize winners?

I doubt they
need this
bear's help!"

"Oh, yes, yes, they need him. The world is

goooooooo big.

They can't
be everywhere
at the same time."

"And the philosophers?" Nosy Fox was growing impatient. "They are the ones with **all the great thoughts** and explanations. Do they need help from Jack the Bear, too?"

"Yes!
Some of
them like to
hide away to think.
They **certainly**
need his help."

"Hmmmmmm..."

Nosy Fox wrinkled his pointy nose. "Don't all the hardworking citizens make the world a better place?"

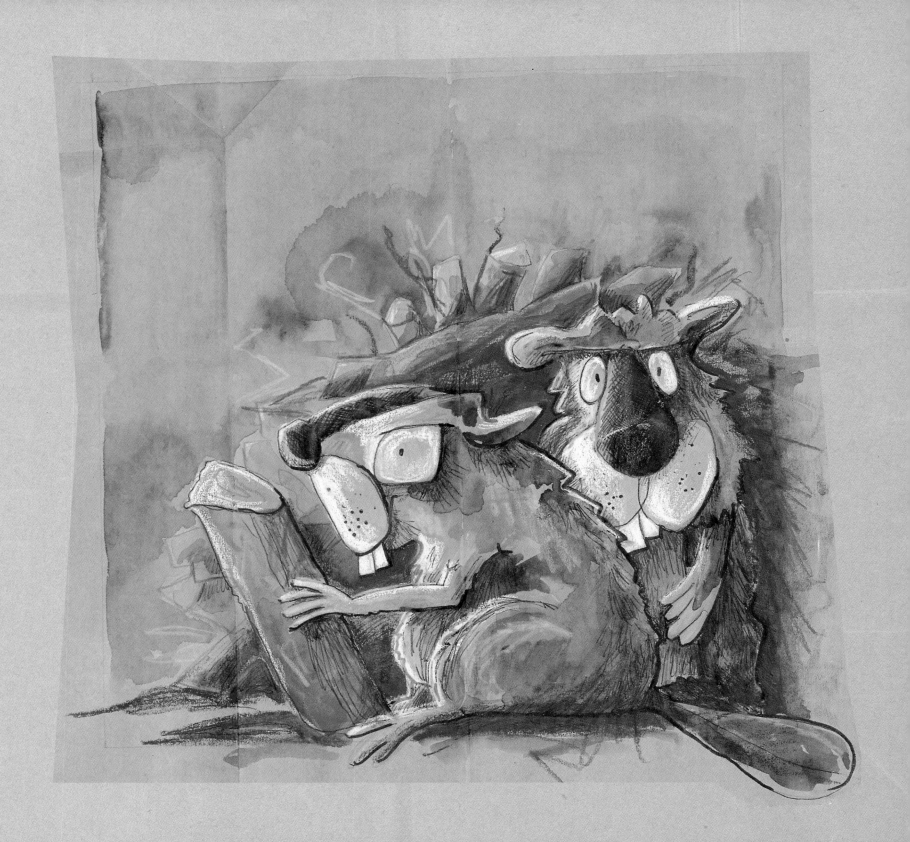

Brainy Owl nodded. "But they often work **too much,** get tired, and then..."

"Maybe... Jack helps out?! **But how?"**

Nosy Fox sighed. "I don't get it! **What** does Jack the Bear **do?"**

"Take a closer look. What's Grumpy Squirrel doing?"

"He's...

he's
smiling!"

"Exactly."

Brainy Owl beamed. "Little good deeds that everyone can do, like making somebody smile, turn the world into a better place."

"Hey, you two!"

Jack the Bear called out. "You've been chatting forever. You must be hungry. Come over here and have some honey."

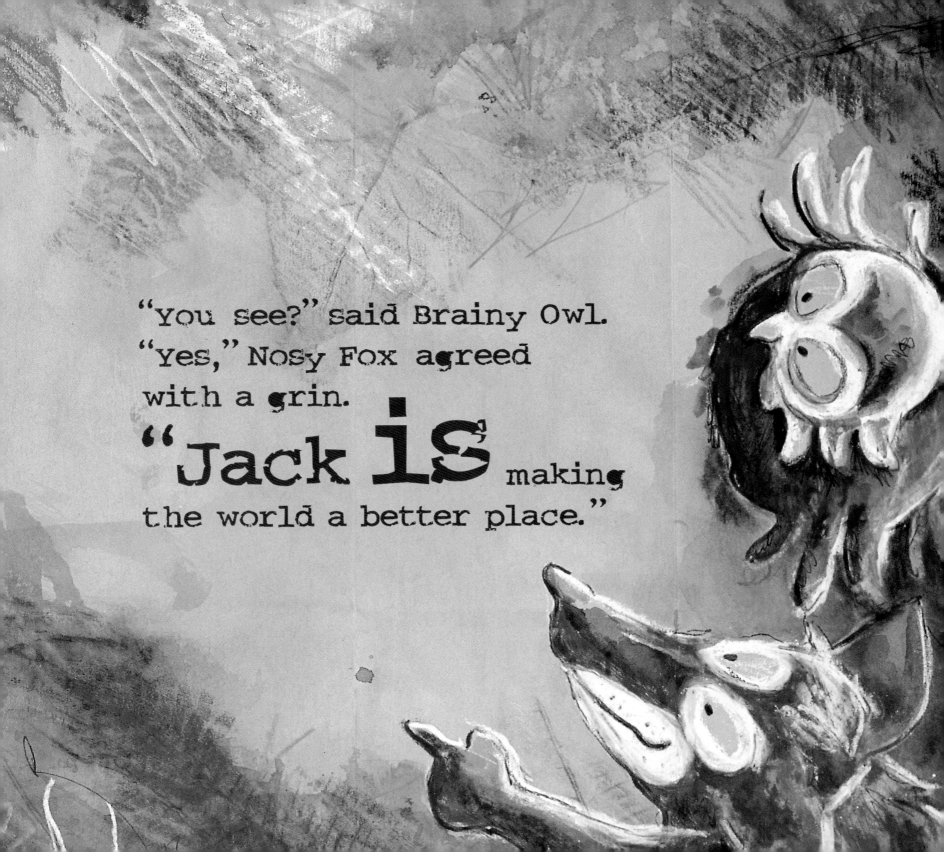

"You see?" said Brainy Owl. "Yes," Nosy Fox agreed with a grin. "Jack is making the world a better place."